Eat the Trees!

Other Wild Food Survival Materials by Linda Runyon

The Essential Wild Food Survival Guide
Linda Runyon's Master Class on Wild Food Survival DVD
Wild Cards
A Survival Acre
Homestead Memories
Why Not LOVE?
Wild Food & Animals Coloring Book
Basic Middle Eastern Desert Survival Guide

Eat the Trees!

Written & Illustrated

by Linda Runyon

A Wild Food Company Publication

Eat the Trees!
August 2011

Published by
the Wild Food Company
Dorchester, Massachusetts

DISCLAIMER

This book is intended to be an educational tool for gathering, storing, and preparing edible tree parts. The information presented is for use as a supplement to a healthy, well-rounded lifestyle. The nutritional requirements of individuals may vary greatly, therefore the author and publisher take no responsibility for an individual using and ingesting tree parts.

State and local regulations on foraging trees vary, but mostly there are restrictions against taking tree parts from public land. You should always check with park officials before foraging anywhere but on your own land. If you know you are, or might be, on private land and wish to forage there, be sure to get the land owner's permission to do so.

All Rights Reserved
Copyright © 2011 by Linda Runyon
Editing, Typesetting & Study Guide by Rosary Shepherd
Cover design & select photos by Eric Conover

ISBN 978-0-936699-25-7

Printed in the United States of America

OfTheField.com

The Wild Food Company
101 Train Street, Suite 1
Dorchester, MA 02122

DEDICATION

Eat the Trees! is dedicated to anyone who realizes the environment of nature is one of the most precious parts of our lives. Without the trees and their contributions to Earth we could not survive as human beings. We who realize this and work to keep the principles alive, do so in the hopes that for many years to come we might enjoy the prospects of free food that the mighty tree provides. From the bark eaters of yesteryear to the explorers of future food supplements, we salute those who enhance our well being through nature.

> Hear the soft whistles
> of sturdy pines
> breathing a gentle wind
> like a sigh of gratitude
> for the breath of life.

Excerpted from the poem "Sound" from *Why Not LOVE?*, by Ken Heitz.

TABLE OF CONTENTS

Dedication … … … … … … … … … … v

Preface … … … … … … … … … … … ix

Introduction … … … … … … … … … 1

Pine … … … … … … … … … … … 4

Birch … … … … … … … … … … … 24

Balsam Fir … … … … … … … … … 34

Maple … … … … … … … … … … … 44

Willow … … … … … … … … … … 52

Beech … … … … … … … … … … 60

Tree Activities … … … … … … … … 65

Foraging Rules for Edible Trees … … 69

Study Guide … … … … … … … … 71

About the Author … … … … … … 85

PREFACE

This book was conceived in the Adirondacks back in the winter of 1974 or 1975. Those winter months were brutal, and one night it was 30 below 0 °F with a wind around thirty miles an hour. That deep freeze blew up 420 mason and atlas jars full of wild food that I had carefully canned and stored deep in a 9 foot pit. Product that had been put up the summer before to take us through the whole winter had oozed onto the shelves amidst the broken glass. That night, as I looked in despair at the ruined food and contemplated how I would feed my family through the cold months ahead, I thought about the many trees nearby. I wondered how I might use them for food in the winter. And thus were planted the seeds for what would eventually become this book.

The first thing I did was to find tree twigs, defrost them, and laboriously grind them to flour. Then I gathered new buds off a limb and fried them in oil and spiced them for a meal. During that long winter I really found out why the Iroquois and Algonquin Indians ate all sorts of trees, and many parts of trees, and how they had survived through harvesting them. While I did have to learn some tough lessons that year, they made me stronger and more able to face the hardships and the joys that make up the game of life. Enjoy!

ACKNOWLEDGEMENTS

Without the skill and dedication of the editor and publisher, a book does not come to fruition. It is with my sincerest thanks that Rosary Shepherd and my son, Eric, have brought my thoughts into the words of this book.

Eat the Trees!

INTRODUCTION

When I was a little girl, lying on my back in the grass and staring up through the branches to the very tippy top of the tall pine tree gently swaying in my yard, I had no idea how important trees would become to my very survival. Circumstances would lead me to realize and appreciate that probably the most useful naturally growing plant on our planet is the tree.

Thank goodness there are all kinds of trees, and fortunately for everybody, that there are so many of them all over the earth! Trees provide shelter, and food, and all kinds of wood and paper products, and you can even make shoes from trees too. Kids love to climb in trees and swing from them into lakes and ponds and rivers.

And there's just nothing like laying back on a wide tree branch and letting your imagination watch the cloud creatures slip across the sky. There are dances, songs and stories for trees, about trees, and with trees, and some of the most beautiful photographs in the world include them. But the most immediate and fundamental survival use of a tree is by people who have the knowledge and willingness to forage (search for food in a natural environment) from a tree and feed themselves from the tree. For free.

This book will discuss five kinds of trees that are found in many parts of the world, and which I include in my book *The Essential Wild Food Survival Guide,* with the addition of beech. I will show how to identify the trees, how to gather food from them, how to make flour and other edible foods from them, along with additional helpful information on other uses. I will tell you some of my own personal adventures with foraging trees, and I've included some specific activities for children at the end of the book. There is also a study guide that provides practical steps for a more thorough understanding of how to forage trees for free food.

White pines

PINE

<u>Other Names</u>: The pine tree has many names, such as: jack pine, pinyon pine (sometimes spelled "pinon"--this is the one that grows the pine nuts that are so delicious!), short-needled pine, white pine. Different species of the pine tree have different Latin names. For example, the Eastern White Pine is *pinus strobus*. Pine trees are considered "conifers" because the way they reproduce is to drop cones that are filled with seeds.

<u>History</u>: The pine tree has been helpful to mankind as far back as we can determine historically, and has several uses. Of particular importance is the pine sap (as a fuel you can burn), pine pitch (created from the pine resin and then boiled down for use to seal the wood in wooden ships), and the inner bark layer can be extracted from the tree, ground to flour and then used in baking. In fact, the Algonquian Indians of upstate New York were given a derogatory name that meant "bark eaters", because when food was scarce, they would eat the inside of the bark of the white pine, and also flavor their food with shredded bark. We know that George Washington ate bread made from pine needles and inner tree bark in his time.

<u>Habitat</u>: Pine trees can be found in many areas, such as dry soil areas, on mountain tops as well as canyon tops, and in moist soils too, like the deep forests throughout the Northwestern areas of the U.S. and Canada. The pinion pine, famous for those pine nuts, can be found in the Middle West and Western states of the U.S. (it is actually the state tree of New Mexico), and in Mexico.

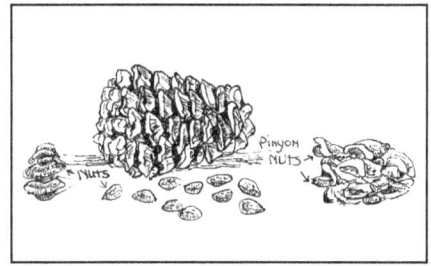

Pine cone and pinyon nuts

<u>Identification Characteristics of the Pine Tree</u>: Pine trees grow needles instead of leaves, and they grow pine cones on their

2 to 5 pine needles per cluster

branches. A way to identify the pine is that the needles are bundled together, usually in clusters of two to five needles. The outer bark of the pine tree is smooth to scaly. Some species of pine tree, such as the white pine, can grow to be 50 to 80 feet tall. (Note: To aid in plant identification, use at least three reference sources that include clear pictures.)

Unlike deciduous trees whose leaves change color in the fall and drop to the ground, pine trees stay "evergreen" during the cold winter months. You can see the tall, stately pine tree visible from a distance—a beacon of strength, faithfulness (our Christmas trees are often pine), and a natural nutritional resource.

Your Foraging Equipment: The pine tree is a treasure trove of goodies for eating once you know how to find and use them. But before I get into specifics about identifying and foraging from the pine tree, here is a list of equipment and materials that I suggest that you bring along on any foraging adventure.

The first item is a backpack that will contain the following for easier transportation:

- cutting tools such as: clippers, a sturdy sharp knife, a hatchet or hand saw for chopping down tree branches, and scissors for clipping off small branches or leaves;

- paper bags or similar containers to drop your food gatherings in once you have harvested them, baggies for smaller items, plastic grocery bags;

- a clean sheet to place edible tree parts onto;
- optional items such as a cell phone, rubber bands, a whistle, notebook and pen, camera, a field guide for identification purposes (for the plants you want to harvest and the ones you need to avoid),
- water, additional food as desired.

In addition to the backpack, you will also want to bring a bigger container like a bucket to take home larger tree parts that will be further processed at home. When on a foraging trip, be sure to wear sturdy shoes and old clothes that you don't mind getting dirty or snagged on bushes and such. Bring thick gloves with you, and a hat would be a good idea, too. Before you leave for foraging, review the "Foraging Rules for Edible Trees" on page 69 of this book.

Edible Parts of the Pine Tree

Catkins: The "catkin" is an edible part of some species of pine tree, such as the white pine, the longleaf pine, the Monterey pine, and the bristlecone pine. Catkins often develop into pine cones if not gathered first for food. Catkins do not look like flowers or needles, but instead look a bit like yellow or tan caterpillars. The catkins can be harvested starting in early spring, and usually through the spring season, but certainly before summer. Catkins can be sticky, so have your gloves on when you go to pick them. You could pick enough catkins from the end of one big tree branch to have a winter's supply of them for food. Catkins are very high in vitamin C, and they (as well as

Catkins on branch

the needles) have been used as an herbal remedy for colds since early times. When I have a cold, I toss a few into a cup of boiling water for a few minutes, strain the water and drink it. Sometimes it is just the ticket for soothing a sore throat. When you eat catkins, a few go a long way in terms of calories. New growth can be used in the same ways as catkins. See pages 23 and 54 for images of new growth before they become needles.

<u>Needles:</u> The pine needles are also edible, and they are on pine trees all year round. You can pull the needles from the branch in bunches and place them in a paper bag separate from your catkins bag. After you get them home, fresh pine needles can be put in a glass jar filled with water and placed out in the sun for a few hours to make tea. Or you can twist a few of the fresh needles and chew in the center for a pine taste. Children especially like to do this because twisting the needles releases the inner liquid for them to taste.

<u>Inner Bark</u>. The wood of trees is made up of different layers.

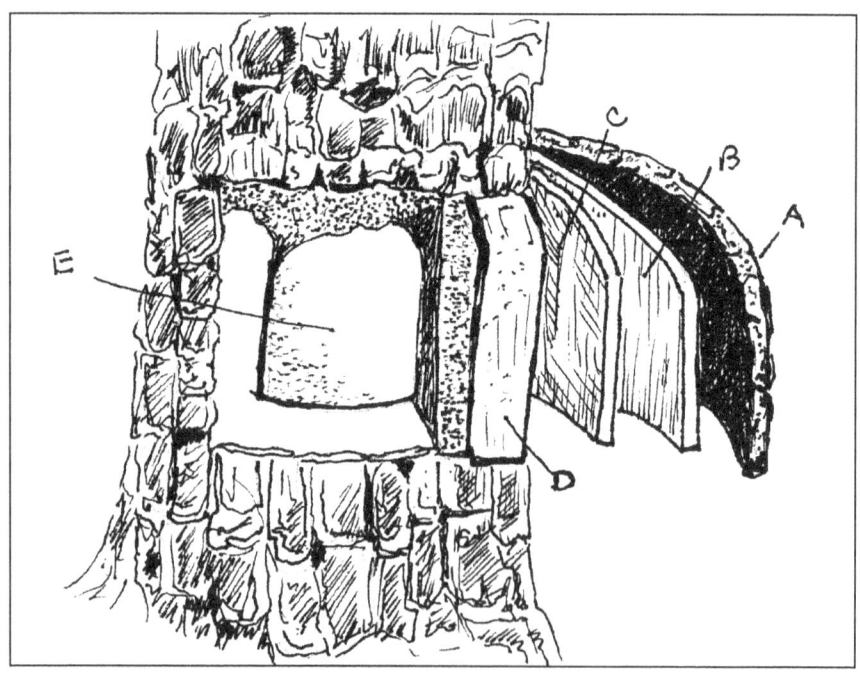

A. Outer Bark B. Inner Bark C. Cambium
D. Sapwood E. Hardwood (core)

The inner bark is the layer that can be harvested and used for food. If you've ever seen cinnamon stick rolls that come from the inner bark of the cinnamon tree, this is exactly the same idea of using the inner bark for food.

The background story of my inner bark adventures starts one winter after I had canned and stored 420 jars of edible wild food I had made the previous summer over a campfire. I stored those jars in a storehouse which during that particular winter got so cold that all but a few of the jars exploded and we were in a real emergency situation for food that winter. I had gathered a little bit of data about harvesting trees for food by that time, but I really educated myself that winter out of sheer survival necessity, and over the years developed my own procedure for harvesting and transporting tree inner bark. Using a hatchet, I cut down a small branch about 4 or 5 inches across at the joint with the tree. Then I peeled the outer bark layer off all around the branch so that I could see the reddish inner bark layer underneath. I put the outer bark rolls in a bucket to take home, because that wood is of terrific use in helping to start the many fires I made over the years. I put the inner bark branches in a different pail to carry home to prepare for food. That was a very important lesson for me, and I learned from it.

Over the years I developed easier methods of harvesting the inner bark. Here's how I got to the inner bark of some smaller pine branches that grow near my house.

Pine branch outer layer peeled

Inner bark peeled

When I was harvesting larger branches (6" or more in diameter) for a longer-lasting and dependable food supply, I figured out a procedure to help me get to that thicker inner bark layer once I had the branch on the ground. First I cut all the way through the branch every 15 inches or so to have manageable tree branch segments. That way I would not have to deal with the entire length of the branch at one time. For each segment I removed the outer bark and got to the inner bark layer. Then I cut through the inner bark layer to the cambium layer. You can tell when you have hit the cambium because it is lighter in color. Next I used my hatchet to separate the inner bark from the cambium for each segment. I then had a number of inner bark roll segments which I put on my sheet that I had spread out on the ground near the tree.

Here are the steps in order:

        1. Saw a low branch off.
        2. Gather needles.
        3. Using hatchet, cut into inner layer.
        4. Gather inner bark sections.
        5. Gather up cones.

Sometimes it was a challenge to cart the larger pieces home, but I knew they would provide me many meals, so I was always able to get them home.

You can certainly forage for pine tree inner bark in warmer weather, but when harvesting from edible trees from 8 to 12 inches in diameter, I found that it was actually easier to do my inner bark collecting in the winter months. The reason is because the inner bark is more dense that time of year when it is frozen. So during a lull in the snow blizzards, I would wade out to the nearest pine tree, for example, chop a frozen branch, and drag it home. I discovered that while the branch is frozen, I could put the blade at the edge of the inner bark layer and start to pry up the inner bark all around the branch. Imagine my surprise when the inner bark separated and popped off the branch in large curved chunks! I can tell you that action really speeds up the whole process.

After a while I also brought home smaller branches and twigs too, because I discovered they had their own particular uses, as I will explain below. I also brought home some pine cones, because they are a good fire starter, and because they are wonderful to have for decorations around the house, especially at Thanksgiving and Christmas.

Survival Tips: A particular survival tip for you (that I learned under somewhat extreme circumstances) is that one time when I was foraging in very cold weather and needed nourishment, I found a pine tree and was able to obtain pine needle juice by twisting some needles (this works for short or long-needled pines) and sucking the juice. (I first washed the needles in the snow.) The taste is a bit milder than the inner bark of that tree. I felt great from that and it satisfied me and I was able to continue on home from one of my "lost times" in the great forest.

On another winter excursion, when I knew I only had 4 or 5 hours before dark and I had to read my own tracks in the snow to find my way home, I munched on dried pine sap, and the sap from balsam and whatever other such trees showed up along the trail back. I also chewed on handfuls of young frozen leaves, and chewed the bark from small, easily broken branches for energy. And so in this way I nibbled and munched my way home to safety.

Spring Foraging: The springtime provides a bit more variety of edible tree foods. Here's a list of pine tree parts that I would bring home on a very successful foraging expedition in the spring:

- a paper bag of catkins
- a paper bag of pine needles
- a large plastic bag of pine cones
- a bucket of outer bark
- a bucket of smaller tree branches
- some large curved segments of inner bark.

I brought the large pieces home in the sheet that I had laid them on after I cut them off the tree branch. Then I would lug the bags, buckets and pails of my bounty home. Sometimes I had transportation, but often I had to get my precious edibles home through my own efforts.

A Note on Tree Roots: You would not ordinarily dig up a tree to get at the roots and harvest them, because it would needlessly kill the tree. However, if you came upon a pine, birch, maple or beech tree that had been uprooted for some reason, you could forage and prepare the inner bark from the exposed roots the same way as you would for inner bark branches.

Storage and Preparation: The catkins should be dried thoroughly and then stored in a glass container so they can be used later. Catkins stored this way stay edible for a long time. I have some that I first stored in a jar 20 years ago and they still have a nice pine taste. You can also freeze some in ice cube trays or freezer containers to make tea with at a later time. The thin inner bark, the small branches and the twigs should be cleaned with a scouring pad, nail brush, or a handy toothbrush.

Some of the smaller branches with needles on them can be placed in two cups boiling water while their scent is still fresh, to make a delicious and nutritious hot tea. Reduce the heat and let simmer for a few minutes, then pour into a glass pitcher and add honey or maple syrup for an excellent pick-me-up. You can also make "sun tea", which you get by putting a couple handfuls of washed pine or balsam fir needles into a glass quart-sized pitcher of clean water, and then let it sit in the sun for a day. Another way to make sun tea is by putting twigs from birch and balsam trees into the water and letting them sit out in the sun. The pine needles themselves can be ground to a mush-type consistency for a hint of pine flavor and nutrition such as in oatmeal, rice or bread pudding, etc.

Once the larger rolls of inner bark have been washed and dried completely, they should be cut down to usable dimensions. With a sturdy knife, cut the bark sections into smaller, more

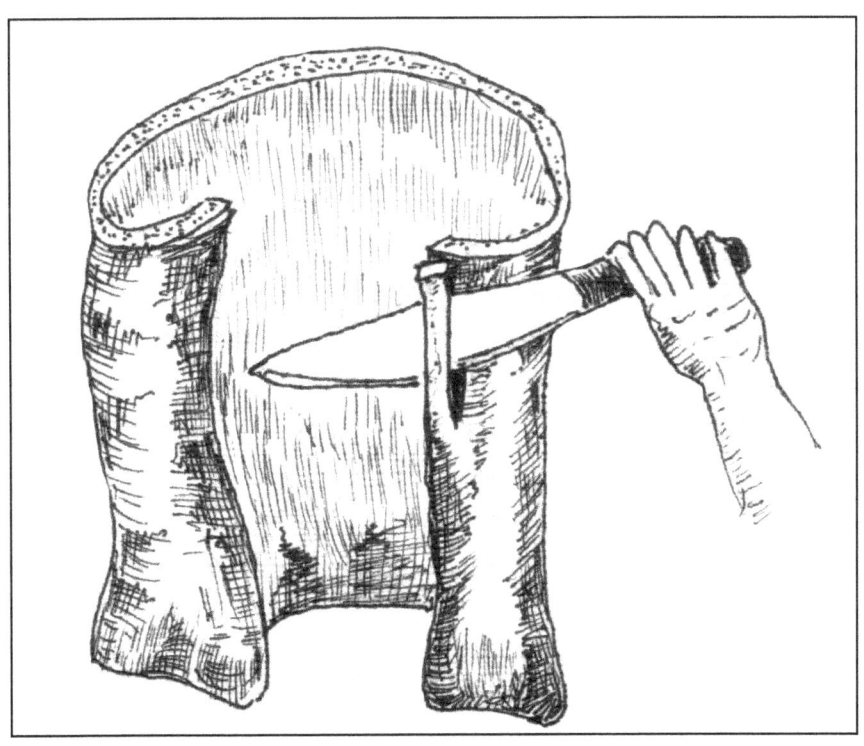

Cutting inner bark strips

manageable strips that are 1″ to 4″ long, about 1″ wide, and about 1/2″ deep that you can dry and store conveniently.

When you are sure they are dried completely, put them in paper bags for storage in a consistently dry place inside the house. Do this too for the twigs, branches and needles. I had a shelf for holding bags of various tree parts, and I labelled what each bag had in it.

Storage bags of twigs, branch sections, needles

Later on, a twig can be stuck into each square of a popsicle tray that is filled with sun tea and maybe a drop of honey and then frozen, for a very different popsicle-on-a-stick that kids will love. If there's any tea left over, just pour it into ice cube containers and when the cubes are frozen, put them into a labeled plastic bag to store in the freezer so you can chill and flavor a drink later on. With the rest of the twigs you can scrape the bark from them and you will get "curls" of bark that can be saved for later, to munch on for a light, nutritious snack. Many times

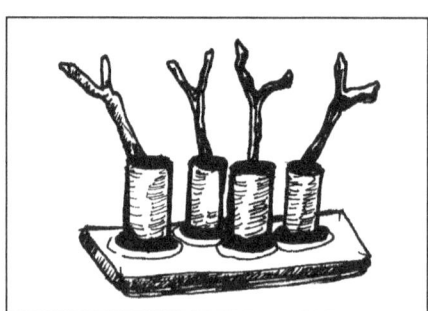
Pine twig popsicle sticks

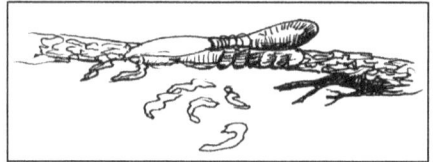
Peeling pine twig curls

I made car trips of 8 hours to visit my daughter while the bark curls dangled from my mouth.

There are many food choices for the thin, dried, crispy inner bark. They are easily nibbled, and 5 or 6 of these stops the hunger pangs quickly when on a mountain climb or out in a canoe, or driving in the car. They can also be added with onions to stir frys (a main meal, stirred over a wood stove years ago), or chopped into cubes to include in salads, or simply fried in oil and added to other dishes of your choice. Here is free food, a lot of fiber, and a chewy experience for everybody! When you want to make a more pungent tea than the sun tea made from pine needles, get out a few pieces of the inner bark, put in water, bring to a boil, and then let it steep for an hour or two. Wonderful. You can use this recipe for the inner bark of birch trees, balsam trees. Don't throw out the inner bark pieces after the first batch because they can be used over and over and still give you a wonderful cup of tea.

This photo shows some pine parts and uses.

A. Needles B. Catkins in jar C. Popsicle sticks
D. Larger twigs for stirrers or fire starters E. Shredded inner bark

A Word of Caution: You can freeze and store tree parts just like you would any other edible plant. However, if you want to store tree parts outside in the freezing winter (like the large inner bark curved sections, or bigger tree branches), there is something I did that I want to tell you about. One of the places where we homesteaded had a shed, and I thought it would be convenient to store some tree branches out there during the winter months, so I wouldn't have to go forage for tree food as often. It gets cold doing that in the wintertime! The branches were fine out there during freezing temperatures, but when we had thaws, and especially when spring came, I found that my formerly frozen tree branches now had black mold (black dot clusters on the wood grain) growing on them.

Storing branches in a shed

The first time I saw that I threw all of the affected branches out. Right then. But then I had another similar episode. This time I had stored some large inner bark curved segments in the shed and brought a good-sized one inside the house. I got a look at it, then started to throw it away too. My husband asked me why I was doing that when I had so arduously harvested it and dragged it home. My explanation met with laughter, and then he took his knife and scraped the wood down until there were no areas of black dots. And I went ahead and used that inner bark sheet for food for us, though I do not recommend this as something that others should do!

My suggestion is that if you are going to store tree food parts outside during winter months, cut them up first and store them in a metal box like the metal cookie containers you see in stores during holiday seasons, or even larger such metal boxes. This keeps the tree parts fresh and also might prevent outside humidity from getting to the wood.

Then when warmer weather starts, transfer the food from metal to paper bags, which are porous and will allow the food to dry naturally. You spent time and energy to get that food, so you want to store it so you can use it for later.

Grinding Inner Bark to Flour: The first piece of equipment you will need in order to convert tree bark to flour is a sturdy grinder. Now I use a heavy duty model, to be sure I can get the bark ground to a fine powder to use as flour. In my homesteading days, when I didn't have electricity, I used a small cast iron meat grinder, which didn't get the bark ground fine enough for my taste. But later on, after I came back to civilization, I wanted something that would produce a finer powder that would be much better than what I could get from that meat grinder. So I tried just about every kind of grinder I could locate that was on the market at the time. I was very glad to come across the Vita-Mixer machine, because that one can grind the inner bark into a powder that actually becomes flour and which you can use to bake with as per my suggestions below.

But if you are going to be in a genuine wilderness or homesteading situation with no electricity and you want to be able to grind inner bark to flour while you are there, I recommend that you try out some hand held grinders before you head out. There may be some new ones on the market, especially heavy duty spice grinders that might possibly be adequate, and there's also a very sturdy one piece rectangular grater called a "microplane/micrograter" currently available that perhaps would grate the bark into a fine enough consistency to be flour. That's going to be an arduous job no matter what, but I suspect you could make it work if you had to. After all, the Navaho used a heavy stone tray and a rock to grind their flour.

Regardless of how you accomplish the grinding of the inner bark, the ground tree flour looks like any other flour but has an eggshell tint to it, and may have some flecks of harmless dark outer bark that got included in the grinding process.

You can figure that four or five strips of the thin inner tree bark will yield approximately one cup of flour. However, tree bark flour (especially pine bark flour) is strong in flavor, so you will want to use only a little bit (start with 1/8 cup) in a regular recipe that calls for flour. That small amount provides a lot of fiber and vitamins, as well as bulk.

Use a non-tree type of flour for the rest of the flour needed. I used ground wheat berries (the kernels of wheat) because they can be purchased in bulk at health food stores, they store well (ground tree flour is good only up to 6 months), and require much less work to grind. What worked for me was to fresh grind wheat berries with some pine inner bark strips thrown in. This became a regular activity for me several times a week.

A number of different flours can be used in combination with inner tree bark flour. I suggest that you experiment to find what intensity of tree flavor you want to experience in your baked foods. You may find that you like a stronger pine flavor in muffins, for example, than you do in bread. Pine, while it does have

Wheat berries, Vita-Mixer, and shredded pine bark to make flour

a more noticeable, somewhat bitter flavor and is higher in calories than other barks, is also the tree that provides greater nutrition than the other edible trees we discuss in this book.

The important point to remember is that grinding flour to use fresh is a good way to improve your overall health. Other cultures such as the Navaho Indians used to grind their flour daily, and tribes in New Guinea would grind their plant mixtures as they needed them.

Gathering Pine Tree Sap: As soon as the spring sun begins to warm the earth, the sap begins to rise up in certain species of tree. You can actually stand next to an evergreen softwood tree (pine, balsam fir, spruce) and over a few days see the clear blisters begin to form on the tree trunk.

I have been gathering sap from trees for many years, even after my homesteading days were over. I am so happy to report that where I live now I have a dripping supply of pine sap every season. Three years ago a tree surgeon had removed three of the lower limbs of a softwood pine tree near my present apartment. The cuts of the saw cut the tree limbs flush with the trunk, and the entire sawed end was weeping sap, about head high for me. I knew it would be so, so easy to collect! I went home and gathered my equipment, which was a glass container and a clean stick (I use chopsticks). I easily scraped the gluey substance and put it in the glass.

For weeks you can approach the tree that has sap blisters every day. Just put the stick under the blister, pull the stick up entirely and place it in the glass container. I have

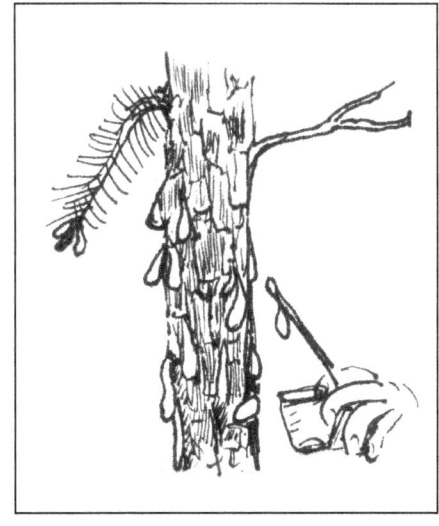

Collecting pine sap

gathered around 2-3 ounces of sap every few weeks easily from this one tree. Children love to poke the blisters and collect pine sap. Our Native Americans revered the blisters as a handy food while on horseback or on foot. One really tasty dessert I developed and made with Jello was that instead of using water as directed on the box, I would substitute a sap solution from pine, birch, or maple. It really did liven up the meal!

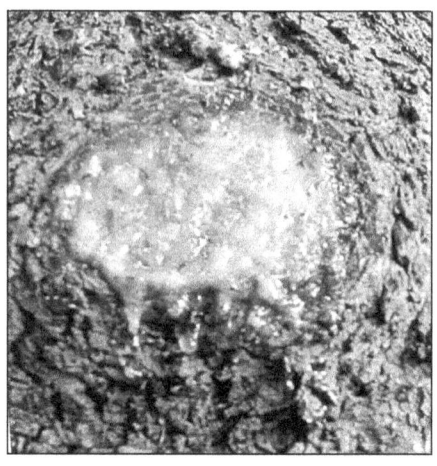

The place where a pine branch was removed

I also like to pull off older pine or balsam fir blisters from a tree and pop them in my mouth because they make the best chewy gum. These blisters are a healthy alternative to commercial chewing gum and if your child swallows that gum, no problem because it's nutritious. Something else to know about the sap from pine and balsam trees is that it will eventually harden and crystalize, much like sugar candy. When it gets hard like that I poke it with a pointed steak knife to make smaller chunks. These pieces of sap candy are great for colds, sore throats, or just for a taste of the forest.

<u>Nutritional Value for Pine Nuts</u> (All Nutritional Chart Data is taken from *The Essential Wild Food Survival Guide*, and is based on data provided by Dr. James Duke):

Amount of nutrient per 100g. (About ½ cup)				Calories: 634	
Water	3.7 g	Calcium	14 mg	β Carotene	20 µg
Protein	15.3 g	Phos.	515 mg	Thiamin	760 µg
Fat	61.3 g	Iron	4 mg	Riboflavin	230 µg
Carbos.	16.8 g	Sodium	72 mg	Niacin	9800 µg
Fiber	2.6 g	Potassium	628 mg		
Ash	2.9 g	Ascorbic.	1 mg		

Nutritional Value for Pine Needles:

Amount of nutrient per 100g. (About ½ cup)				Calories: 141	
Water	51.5 g	Calcium	186 mg	β Carotene	5652 µg
Protein	3.1 g	Phos.	57 mg	Thiamin	110 µg
Fat	4.5 g	Iron	2.7 mg	Riboflavin	240 µg
Carbos.	39.9 g	Sodium	40 mg	Niacin	900 µg
Fiber	14.1 g	Potassium	382 mg		
Ash	1.0 g	Ascorbic.	68 mg		

A Word of Warning!

I did tell you that pine needles are volatile. This is because of certain natural resins in the needles themselves. And here is how I really found out that fact for myself the hard way, as was usual for me. At one time, I ran a craft co-op with the women and men of the town I lived in. Among other craft items, we made pillows filled with dried balsam needles that could be sold in many New York store outlets. People love pine and balsam pillows because they are reminded of the forests and mountain camps as they fall asleep or spend time in their living rooms.

It took time to get the needles sufficiently dried and so one time we thought we could hurry up the drying time by using a microwave to dry out the needles. Don't ever, ever do this! The town had a local diner, which owned a microwave, and so we asked permission to use it. The time we chose, to make matters worse, was during the lunch hour when the diner was quite full of people eating. I had a bag of pine needles in a paper bag and set them in the microwave for a small amount of time. Huge mistake, because BOOM! The door of the microwave blew off, with a rush of flame and smoke pouring out. People were yelling and rushing around in panic. A state trooper who fortunately happened to be eating his lunch there grabbed a fire extinguisher and put out the fire. Thank goodness he was there because I was in so much shock I didn't even see the fire extinguisher.

Let me tell you, this was the one and only very expensive experiment of microwave drying of any softwood needles. I never used a microwave again to dry needles, and I urge you not to ever try it either! It became a moot point, though, when I realized that balsam fir needles would make better pillows, and there's a story about that in the next chapter.

The result of drying pine needles in a microwave!

Other Pine Tree Uses: One particular advantage of the pine tree is that its wood is not as hard as some other trees and is easy to saw, and so is used to build homes and furniture. There are some stories in my book *Homestead Memories* about how we constructed and sold furniture pieces built from the wood of various tree parts collected from our nearby Adirondacks sawmill years ago. Here is a drawing I did of my beautiful coffee table that my husband Ken made for me from one such pine piece.

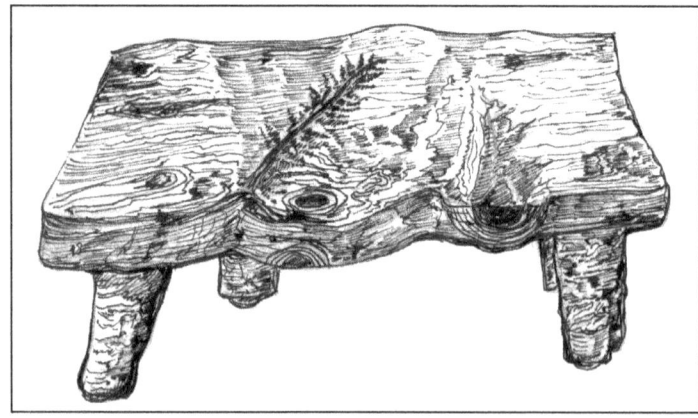

My beautiful hand-made pine table

Another use of pine has to do with the root. The early settlers made rope from pine roots. One pine tree can have roots yards and yards long. The pioneers would find a felled tree and dig to the end of the root. These tough roots could be sliced in half and used, or used whole if the root was a smaller diameter. Legend has it that the roots were so strong they could pull a wagon. I tried making something useful with pine root and created a very tough, heavy large hamper basket from spliced roots. At one point I did make a rope sturdy enough that it probably could have pulled a car! The hamper I made was later sold to the New York City Folk Art Museum on one of our trips to the "City" to sell the twig furniture we had made.

Medicinal Uses: Another important use of a specific kind of pine tree is medicinal. There is a European coastal pine tree of the species *Pinus Maritima*, whose bark has been found to be very helpful. The trade name for this bark is Pycnogenol, and you can get information about it on the internet, and at your local health food store, which is very likely to carry this valuable product. Another possible medicinal use of pine is to make a cough syrup from the white pine sap. Be sure to research this yourself for more information on this.

Early pine growth

Birch tree

BIRCH

Other Names: White birch, paper birch, yellow birch, golden tree, black birch, river birch. There are many different kinds of birch trees. The Latin name for the species of tree that is birch is the *betula* species.

History: Since the wood of the birch tree is so sturdy, its first historical use was probably for shelter, and then for canoes for water transportation. Other early uses of birch were for making utensils, equipment like buckets, items that required a strong type of wood. Early on, Mankind figured out that the bark of the birch tree is highly flammable and so the birch bark became the staple wood for starting fires. The Cree Indians in Canada may have created a form of paper using birch bark, and with which they could create designs by biting on the paper. Other Native American Indians used birch bark paper to make charcoal drawings on. It is likely that soldiers during the Civil War were fed birch pulp as a food source when nothing else was available, thus saving many lives.

Habitat: Birch trees in general are found where there are cool, moist soils and where they can get the full sunshine on their leaves. There are birch trees found in many countries, and you can find a species of birch just about anywhere on the North American continent.

Identification Characteristics of the Birch Tree: The small, greenish flowers of the birch tree appear in early spring before the leaves begin to grow. The leaves of birch trees have short stems, and "toothed" edges. Birch trees are known for their papery bark, especially the white birch. The bark of the white and paper birch peels in curls.

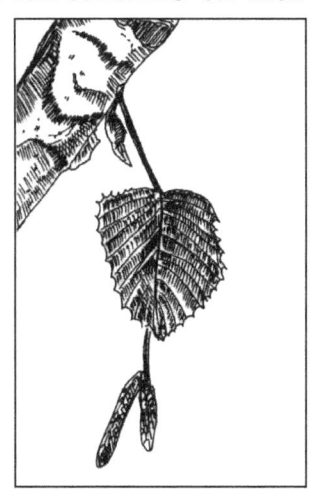

Birch leaf and 2 catkins

Edible Parts of the Birch Tree

<u>Birch Catkins and Buds:</u> Birch catkins and buds (which grow into leaves) are found on the trees in early spring.

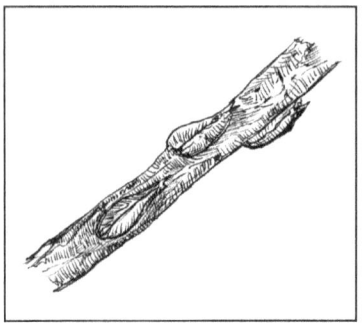

New bud forming on branch

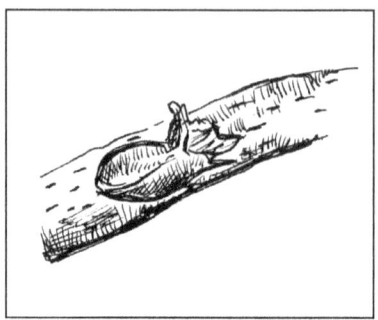

New leaf starting growth

Other edible parts include (similarly to the edible pine parts): twigs, branches, inner bark and sap. Caution: Be careful to only eat small amounts of these birch parts at one time, less than 1/2 cup certainly of the catkins and buds, only a few twigs, a small amount of flour. This is because there is a substance that can be isolated from the birch tree which is called acetylsalicylic acid, and which is the active ingredient in aspirin. In fact, the reason I first started to harvest birch catkins and buds was because I once saw a logger pull a birch branch down and nibble one bud after another until he had eaten about 1/4 cup of them. He told me the tree had aspirin in it and that he felt better after eating those buds. And so that's how I learned how to do that too. When you harvest the edible parts of the birch tree, do it the same way as you would for pine. You can cut off a birch tree branch,

Logger nibbling birch buds

or find a birch branch on the ground, or harvest an entire tree that has blown over or blown down.

One frigid winter day I came upon a white birch that had a big broken branch off the main trunk and was lying in the snow. There were 12 inches of snow on that broken branch. I knew that one branch contained several winter's worth of inner bark for birch tea, and for flour, so I was all set to harvest it, even in the cold. And it was with a frozen birch tree that I found out what I said in the pine tree chapter about how much easier it is to separate the inner bark layer in cold weather. That was a good foraging day for sure, and it added to my supply in my little upright freezer I used to have outside to keep the bears out. That freezer contained labeled bags of stored edibles and supplies for a quick pot of tea or soup, and whenever my friends came by during the winter I would already have their favorite one ready to pull out and make a nice hot pot of tea for our visit, plus a fragrant and warming bowl of wild soup.

Collecting Birch Sap: Collecting birch sap is different from poking pine blisters because the birch sap is much thinner than that of pine sap and just drips down the tree if a branch is cut off from the trunk. The method I developed for collecting birch sap is based on the way earlier Native Americans did it, but I altered it a bit for current times.

Tapping birch sap

Here's how I "tapped" a birch tree: I would make a 3 foot vertical measure from the ground up the tree trunk and mark that spot. At that mark I would make a horizontal cut through the outer bark about

27

3 1/2 inches long. Using that cut as the top line of a square, I outlined, cut out, and removed a rectangle of outer bark 3 1/2 inches square. That way I had cut out the rough outer bark and had a smooth surface of inner bark. Then I would drill a hole 3 or 4 inches into that square and into the sapwood layer. I then inserted a hollow "spile", which is a hollow plug that provides a channel for the sap to flow out from the tree.

I made mine from wood such as slippery elm, about 5-6 inches long, 2 inches wide and curved on the surface. I would then attach a bucket to the spile and then wait for the sap to flow into it. I found that birch sap will drip through the spile at the rate of a quart to a gallon for the better part of a spring day. I have known people to use all sorts of things to make their spiles, including plastic handles of a Clorox bottle, or even trombone mouthpieces! Whatever works to serve as a channel from the inner sap to the bucket.

Sap flows from April through June, and I could generally be certain to obtain a gallon a day during that time. For birch, as soon as the birch buds begin to break, the sap season is essentially over. Birch sap then gets cloudy and the taste changes noticeably.

Because birch sap is thin and watery, it could take hundreds of gallons of sap to boil down to one gallon of birch syrup. This is probably why you don't often see bottles of birch syrup for sale alongside other kinds of syrup. If you wanted birch molasses, that would take even more birch sap boiled down.

Once when I climbed a mountain with my husband and we forgot our water supply, we broke branches off a white birch tree and for 20 minutes were able to quench our thirst from the sap that was available. We did the same thing on our way down, until we got to a stream and were able to drink from that water supply.

Nutritional Value for Birch Leaves:

Amount of nutrient per 100g. (About ½ cup)				Calories: 1	
Water	88.0 g	Calcium	186 mg	β Carotene	5652 μg
Protein	3.3 g	Phos.	57 mg	Thiamin	110 μg
Fat	1.0 g	Iron	2.7 mg	Riboflavin	240 μg
Carbos.	6.7 g	Sodium	40 mg	Niacin	900 μg
Fiber	2.0 g	Potassium	382 mg		
Ash	0.9 g	Ascorbic.	68 mg		

Birch Firewood: Birch wood is really excellent to use for fire wood in your fireplace. When you harvest birch wood for your various edible parts, also be sure to collect some for your fireplace. If you don't care much how it looks in your fireplace, then go ahead and bring home the chunks of birch that remain after you've harvested the inner bark, twigs, etc. It may need to be stacked outside to dry for a time.

Birch logs stacked for winter

However, if you prefer to see the beauty of white birch logs stacked outside your home for the winter month's heat, and if you want to experience the papery outer bark as it burns, then be sure to bring home log-sized pieces of unharvested white birch.

Stack your logs outside. The white outer bark "skin" of the tree, the paper part, will help to protect the wood for many seasons and will still be there after the wood inside has rotted out! This is when I have been known to skin off that outer layer and use it for inside tinder to start a fire in my fireplace, or to draw on. Many drawings on white birch "skin," with charcoal as the pencil, sold in the neighborhood lake store where I lived. I loved doing a collection of drawings of trees, cabins and lakes, etc. They seemed to sell fast to the tourists who frequented the shops of Adirondack souvenirs.

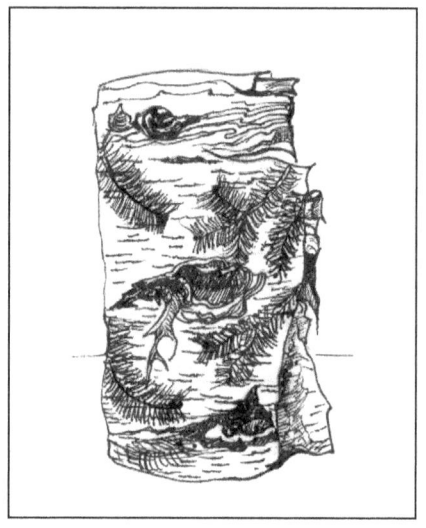

Birch bark souvenir drawing

I still have a beautiful piece of birch bark that is off a log and mostly intact. It is about 8 inches in diameter, and about a foot tall. It sits on my armoire, and some day I will draw something wonderful on it. I have some ideas of what I might want to do. Birch really did appeal to my artistic soul and I found another way to include it into my drawings that I could

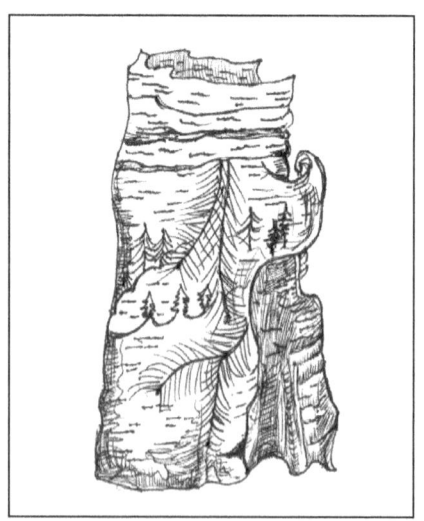

Imaginary birch bark scene

share with others. I was able to get birch disks cut about an inch thick using a certain blade on the saw that made the wood surface smooth as silk. That gave me a small wood "canvas" on which to ink in various scenes, whatever suited my fancy at

the time. Sometimes I sprang for a can of shellac that sealed the permanent ink drawing in. These also were good souvenir sellers at the lake shore store. People loved using them for coasters when they got home, memories of their trip to the Adirondacks.

Drawings on birch disks

Birch Survival Strips: Something else you can do with birch that you could show and involve children in is the following: Bring home branches of birch about 2 inch or less in diameter. When you are ready to do this demonstration with the children, introduce the project to them by giving them some data about harvesting trees. Show them a piece of a birch branch, and identify the outer bark layer. Explain that the birch outer bark is really handy when you are starting and maintaining a campfire. Then remove the twigs and stems from the branch (and save them for munching on later), but be careful to leave the outer bark layer itself untouched as much as you can.

Cut the branch into pieces that are about 6 inches long. Take one piece and cut through the outer bark down to the inner bark layer. Separate the outer bark layer from the rest of the branch so that you have a curve segment of the outer bark of that branch. Set the rest of the branch aside (for a possible demonstration of inner bark and its

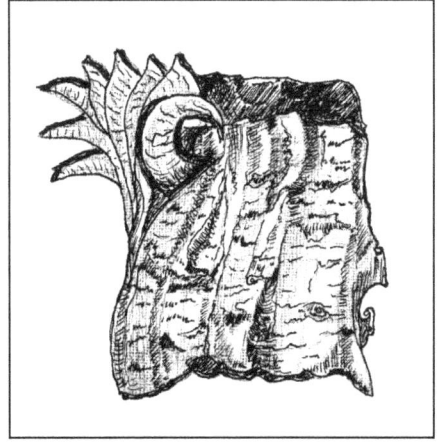

Separating birch bark layers

potential as flour). Then carefully peel off a thin layer of the papery outer bark all the way around the branch. You should end up with a piece of thin outer bark that is 6 inches long and as wide as the the section is long, which you show the children. If a person (or child) does it carefully, one could peel off perhaps 8 or more thin outer birch layers this way.

For all of the birch branch pieces that you have, remove the entire outer bark layer from each one and hand that curve of bark to each child. Offer a prize for the one who can peel off many thin layers within a specified period of time while ensuring that each layer is in one piece. Otherwise you'll get tatters of bark all over the place! Award the winner, and then use scissors to show the children how to cut the bark into strips that are each about one inch wide and 6 inches long. When they have cut their strips of outer bark and have a pile of them, show the children how to wind each strip up so that one end can be tucked up into itself into a little packet. These the children should keep as part of their personal survival pack.

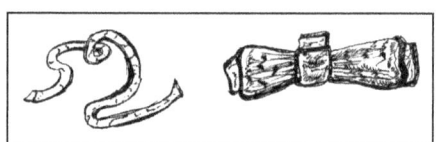

Birch bark strip and packet

As they learn about surviving outdoors, and perhaps in the wilderness, they will realize the value of these little packets they have with them, because these little birch pieces in particular are very good for helping to get a nice, warm campfire going that will last for a while.

<u>Other Birch Tree Uses</u>: Chewing on a birch twig while working will give you a hint of sap flavor, plus a bit of natural aspirin that many people find is very soothing for them. A commercial drink made from distilled birch sap is a carbonated drink called "birch beer" that tastes similar to root beer, and the natural sweetener Xylitol comes from the bark of the birch tree. Research has suggested that birch sweeteners may not cause cavities. And on the other end of the birch spectrum, the bark of the black birch is high in betulin, which has many uses from medicinal to

cosmetic. In the wood industry, birch is considered to produce the strongest plywood, and sturdy Norwegian boats are often built from birch.

Medicinal Uses: Paper birch has paper-like outer bark. This paper bark may be soaked in water for some time, becoming supple and moldable. Wrapped around an affected limb, it makes a quite proper dried cast. "Oil of wintergreen", or methyl salicylate, was originally made from birch as a by-product of the wood industry.

Birch catkins

Balsam fir tree

BALSAM FIR

Other Names: Christmas tree, eastern fir, blister pine (because the sap blisters much like the pine tree sap). The Latin for the North American species is *Abies balsamea*.

History: Balsam has been used for thousands of years as a medicinal oil (made from the tree resin) for respiratory problems like the flu, and as an ointment for muscle pain. Balsam is mentioned many times in the Bible, and some believe that the "liquid gold" mentioned in it is probably balsam oil. The oil has many different kinds of uses, ranging from perfume and soaps to household cleaners.

An ointment made from balsam fir resin was used in the Civil War on wounds received in combat because of its healing properties. And then of course, the balsam fir has had quite an illustrious history as the traditional tree that is decorated at Christmas time. Many "Christmas tree" farms have sprung up world wide to meet the demands of that holiday season.

Habitat: The balsam tree grows best in cooler climates with well-drained soil and a lot of moisture.

Identification Characteristics of the Balsam Tree: A softwood evergreen tree, the balsam fir has small, short needles that grow alternately from under the stem, 1 to 1 1/2 inches long. The tree itself grows to a height of 40 to 60 feet and is found throughout Canada and the United States, and other parts of the world that have cooler climates.

The bark of a young balsam fir is an ash-gray color and relatively smooth. There are horizontal bumps on the surface

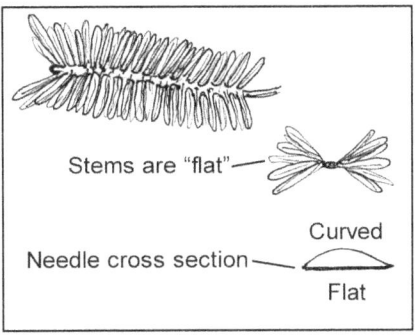

Balsam fir needle cross section

35

of the trunk which are filled with the very sticky sap. These are the blisters.

Balsam bark on a large tree showing the blisters

Balsam cones pointing to the sky

The cones on a balsam stick straight up and are 4 to 6 inches long. You'll never find one on the ground though, because they break up and come down in pieces with the seeds. The core can stay on the tree for years.

Edible Parts of the Balsam Fir Tree

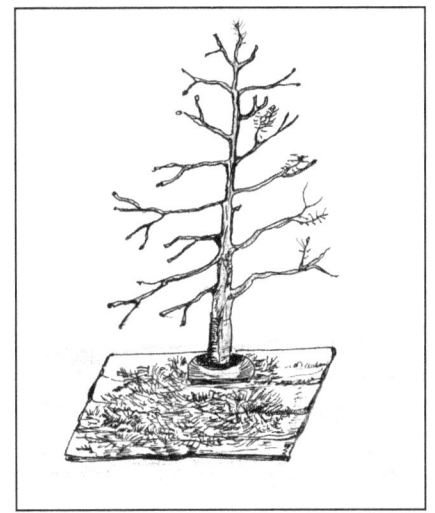
Needles from Christmas tree

Needles and Twigs: The needles and the tips of the twigs can be harvested and ground into flour for storage and use later. Balsam needles can be collected and used in a hot balsam holiday tea, and as a sun tea. I used to wait until some time in January, after my balsam or pine Christmas tree was really bone dry (which I could tell by snapping the little end-twigs) and the needles had started falling off the tree. I would then put a sheet or tarp under the tree and, wearing gloves, pull the needles off the branches so they fell onto the sheet.

All of those needles would be collected and stored in a paper bag for a few weeks. They could stay in the bag for a very long period of time. But if you wanted to store your tree needles in glass containers so you have them for years, be very sure the needles are completely dried first.

One way to be sure any harvested food item is completely dry for storage is to preheat your oven to 200 degrees. When it has reached that temperature, turn the oven off. Then put your wild food in the oven and let it sit there for 5 minutes getting dried out. After that time the food should be thoroughly dried, and after it has cooled completely you can store it. If you purchase your pine or balsam Christmas tree and plan to use it for food after the holiday season, be sure to get one that has not been sprayed with insecticides or other toxic chemicals. Chances are you may want to get an organically grown tree, just to be on the safe side.

In the spring, sap will start to flow in the balsam fir tree. That sap is similar to pine sap except that it is thicker. The pine sap is a bit runny and will drip down the trunk of the tree, but the balsam sap does not. The balsam sap does blister and is very sticky. You can pull it off to have balsam chewy gum, and you can collect the sap and let it crystalize into candy like pine sap, but it takes longer than the pine sap to harden.

Grinding Balsam Wood to Flour: Balsam wood can be ground into flour but I did not do this as often as I did with pine or birch. This is because balsam branches are generally not as big in circumference, which means the wood layers are so very much thinner, often only paper thin. So what I did was to cut off a smaller branch from a balsam fir and bring the whole branch home. I stripped off the needles and set them aside for tea, and I ground the branch itself into flour.

Stripping the needles

But then when I found how pungent the flour was, I decided that my preference in tree flour was with the pine and birch and didn't use balsam for flour much at all. However, when I did find a sizable balsam fir branch, I did process the inner bark and cambium layers into strips for balsam-flavored stir fry (using only a couple of strips), and to save for munching on later, like I did with my pine strips. In fact, to this day I enjoy chewing on a juicy young branch of pine or balsam.

From Trees to Edible Wreaths: Of course pine and balsam branches make excellent and fragrant holiday wreaths, and I created many of them, even before I became aware of the uses of those trees for food. So it became particularly enjoyable to craft wreaths that would be not only festive

but nutritious as well. As I became more knowledgeable about wild edibles, I would make wreaths in which I would work in edible flowers and grasses (as discussed in *The Essential Wild Food Survival Guide*), along with the basic pine or balsam branches and cones. They were some of my favorite gifts for the season, and those of my friends who understood about wild foods were very delighted to receive them.

After the holiday season was long over and I was ready to take down the Christmas wreaths and use them for food, I first pulled out any ornaments or decorations, fabrics, bows, flowers, etc., from the wreaths and saved them for future use. When I was down to just the edible tree parts, and especially if I'd left the wreath up for a while or used it for consecutive winter seasons, I would make sure to rinse the tree parts thoroughly under water to get rid of any dust that may have settled on them. After that I then of course made my own post-holiday teas and other tree food items from the wreaths. The holiday wreaths have been some of my most treasured pleasures of what you can do with edible wild foods.

Nutritional Data for Balsam Fir Needles:

Amount of nutrient per 100g. (About ½ cup)				Calories: 35	
Water	88 g	Calcium	186 mg	β Carotene	5652 μg
Protein	2.8 g	Phos.	57 mg	Thiamin	110 μg
Fat	0.5 g	Iron	2.7 mg	Riboflavin	240 μg
Carbos.	6.5 g	Sodium	40 mg	Niacin	900 μg
Fiber	1.3 g	Potassium	382 mg		
Ash	2.1 g	Ascorbic.	64 mg		

The Smell of the Forest

I still lived in the homestead when I discovered an interesting additional post-seasonal use for the balsam Christmas tree. As mentioned, when dried naturally, the needles came off the twigs easily and the end twigs broke off in the process. So my home town, as a group, chose to make balsam pillows for extra income. My job was not sewing, but gathering enough balsam needles without using ovens, or microwaves for drying (we'd already learned that lesson thoroughly!). The needles were sewn in hundreds of balsam pillows and sold in boutiques in NYC.

We had a lot of needles that needed to be dried completely, so we brought in an 18-wheeler's trailer bed to town and parked it down near a river, away from town so as to be as safe as pos-

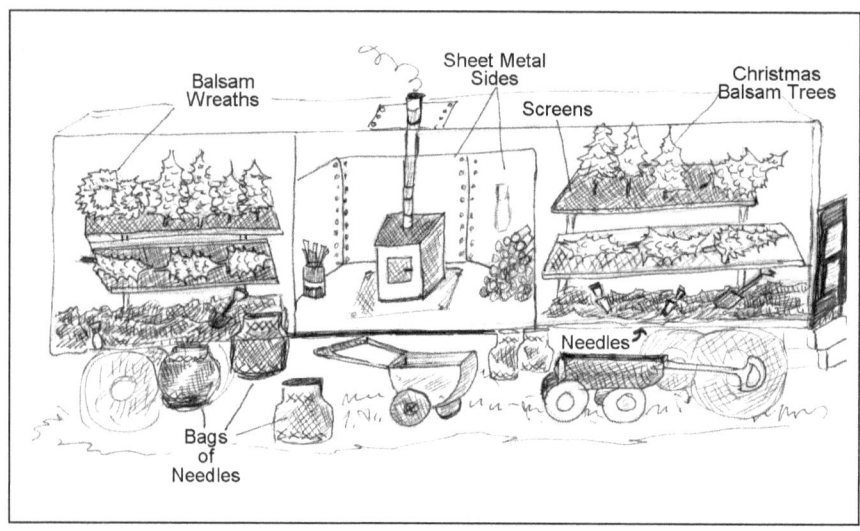

Drying balsam needles to stuff in pillows

sible. Because, in that trailer we had layers of screens bolted onto the steel, double-lined walls, and we also had a very tiny wood stove.

The townsfolk brought their stripped trees and put them into big bins that we had set up outside the trailer. We then stuffed whole trees onto the screens and let the needles dry properly. That little stove only needed about one or two pieces of wood in order to get the needles as dry as we needed them to be for the pillows. We

Our balsam pillow

made sure to get the set-up passed by the town fire department, so we figured we had all bases covered. Hundreds of pounds of needles were gathered and all the people who could sew made extra money when the NYC orders started rolling in. We actually made and sold 200,000 pillows in a 2 week deadline.

While we were doing this we were competing with a company in Maine that was making the same thing and selling their pillows to Lake George, NY, promoting them as "the smell of the forest". We all had very interesting and fun-filled days until we learned that what we were doing wasn't exactly legal. I had no idea I was "running a cottage industry." When asked why I did not have the pillows made in Taiwan for much cheaper cost, I answered, "But I did this for all of us not to have to go on welfare and food stamps in a typical Adirondack winter."

We all learned a lot about balsam needles, we made some extra money, and for sure we learned something about the law. We did, in the end, close down our business to comply with the law.

Winter Camping Survival

Camping in the winter has its own challenges, the cold being the main one. The very first action when setting up camp in the winter is to get a fire started, and sometimes we had to resort to our birch pacquettes that we carried in our backpacks. But most of the time there were evergreens around us. We were able to locate pole-like branches of softwood that were dried and dead, and I was able to strip off the smaller twigs and branches from them to use for

Camping in the snow

kindling. We soon had a hearty fire going and got some hot and warming pine or balsam tea made.

Next thing was shelter, and for that we already had the framework for the best teepee type of shelter that could be erected in a hurry—those dried and dead softwood poles. Add to them some smaller blown-down branches for coverage and there you are. Now for food. The hunt for available winter food included digging down along the edges of big rocks in search of frozen greens that were edible, and also tracking the prints left by deer who might have found frozen greens like wintergreen that grow under the snow. I became skilled at foraging for wild plant food during our winter camping excursions.

There were many times while I sat outside my balsam teepee next to our winter campfire, sipping a warm, fragrant mug of tea, that I truly appreciated the survival skills I had learned over the years.

Other Balsam Fir Uses: You can find uses for balsam fir that include such variety as a non-toxic rodent repellent, and for use in preserving microscopic samples. If you have a stale house odor and want to replace it with a fresh forest scent, place a dab of balsam sap on the pilot light cover of your stove or in a small simmering pot and enjoy the results. The resin blisters from Canada balsam are processed into canoe and boat caulk, and as a waterproof cement. I knew the finest canoe builder in the Adirondacks, and he used balsam pitch on his canoes. To this day his canoes are displayed in the Adirondack museum.

But perhaps one of the most rewarding personal uses for balsam fir is that when the winter holiday season approaches, you can decorate a balsam fir that lives near you. I loved doing that, and over the years I would attach food items like apples to the branches of my trees, in case any wandering birds might need some winter sustenance.

Medicinal Uses: When I was a teenager I worked at a summer

camp as one of a staff of six people. The camp hosted hundreds of people during the summer. On the first day of camp on that particular summer, the owner and all the staff played in the lake to relax. I had a favorite dock that I liked to dive from, but this time when I came up there was a broken bottle that was jammed on my wrist.

When I pulled it out there rushed a gush of blood. The camp was some distance away from the nearest doctor but fortunately the camp owner knew what to do. First he applied a bandage pressure, then he ran to a balsam tree. He poked his penknife into a balsam blister, gathered the very sticky sap onto the blade and swiped the sap onto my wound and "glued the area shut". Fortunately no major vein or artery was cut, and the wound healed up in a few days.

Applications of balsam sap for such injuries became part of our first aid procedure before deciding if there needed to be the long trip to the nearest town for a doctor.

Christmas balsam fir

A row of maple trees

MAPLE

Other Names: Sugar, silver, soft, rock, paperbark, and red maple. Maple trees are in the *Aceraceae* family, with maple sugar trees being the specie *Acer Saccharum,* the best specie for tapping sweet sap to make into maple syrup. The word "Acer" comes from a Latin word that means "sharp", referring to the points on the maple leaf. Maples such as the silver, black, red and paperbark maple can also be tapped for syrup.

History: Making maple syrup was an early spring activity for American natives, who would make a cut in the trees and collect the sap as it dripped. Then they would boil it down, possibly by dropping heated stones into the sap. It is reckoned that maple syrup is probably the first type of commercial food made in this country, and that the Indians traded it to the first European settlers when they arrived. The Chippewa Indians made what they called "maple cakes" by pressing maple seeds into cakes. Maple bedroom furniture was made in colonial American because maple is strong, doesn't split easily and is smooth when polished. This continues to be true today.

Habitat: The maple tree is commonly found in the Northern Hemisphere in temperate regions and on tropical mountain slopes. There are some species that are found in Asia, such as the three-flower maple. Maple trees grow best in soil that is deep, well-drained and moist. Black maple can be found near rivers, and red maple can be found in dry and swampy areas.

Identification Characteristics of the Maple Tree: Maple is a deciduous tree, and generally the leaf has five pointed lobes, are irregular toothed, and are opposite on branches.

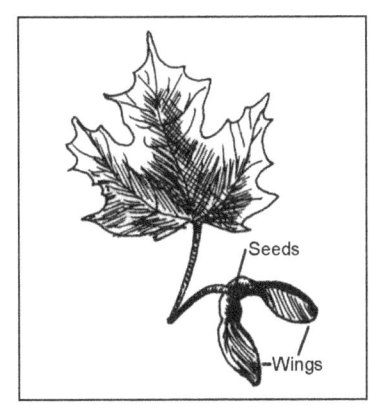

5-point maple leaf and wings

45

Leaves turn golden yellow to scarlet in the fall. The seed is encased in a ball in the middle of two "wings". These wings (also called "whirlybirds" or "helicopters") help the wind to carry the seed away from the parent tree so the new maple will grow up far enough away from the parent. Maple trees generally grow to a height of 20 to 30 feet, though some species grow taller than that. Seeds are ripe when they're brown and down.

Edible Parts of the Maple Tree

<u>Maple Buds and Leaves</u>: Pick the early leaf buds as soon as they start sprouting. I would harvest them as soon as they started to appear on the maple trees in early spring. You can eat the buds right from the tree, or take them home to store them in the freezer for eating later on in a stir fry, for example. Young maple leaves can be picked and added to salads.

<u>Maple Seeds</u>: The maple seeds are found in the helicopters mentioned above. They make really good cakes. I harvested as many of the seeds as I could, probably in the hundreds. I made maple tea by boiling 1/2 cup of seeds in 1 cup of water and then letting the tea steep for 5 minutes. Add a little maple syrup and what a wonderful hot drink in the middle of winter! You can also make maple tea with twigs harvested from the tree and stored in paper bags, same as with other edible twigs, and these twigs are also wonderful for munching on later.

Here's how you get the seeds out of the helicopter wings. First collect the wings into a pile. Then cut the seeds from the wings.

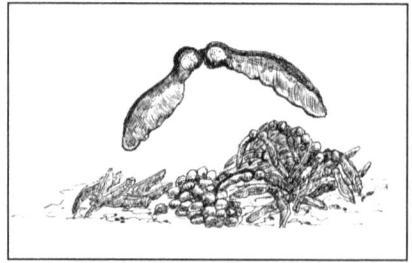

Pile of maple seed wings

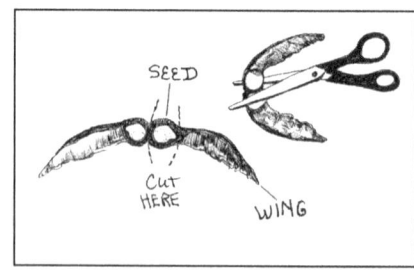

Seeds cut from wings

When you have the seeds separated from the wing, you can just pinch on the seed and it should shoot right out. The seeds will be about the size of a small lima bean. Once you have collected all the seeds from the wings, you can discard the wings.

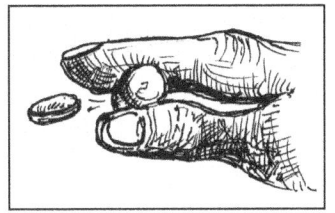

Shooting the seed out

I always used up my maple seeds in seed cakes, but you might want to try roasting them for a snack, or storing them in the freezer for use later on.

Maple Seed Cake Recipe: Take two cups of maple seeds and pound them until they are squishy. With clean hands, make thin patties that you fry in some olive oil or canola oil. Fry both sides until they are brown, then serve with a bit of maple syrup on them. Really a nice treat for us.

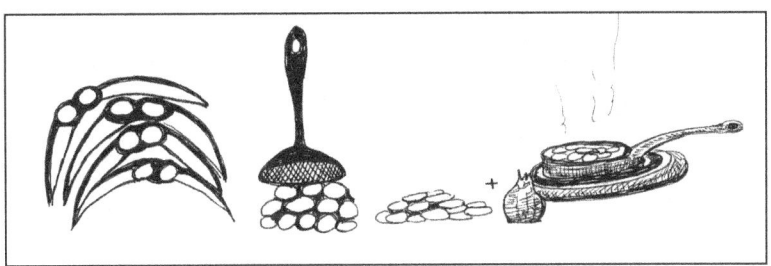

From seeds to cakes

The Maple Sap Saga

I found out the hard way that tapping for maple sap is a long, hard, messy, sticky process. But we didn't know and we had maple trees around and we figured, Why not? So Ken and I went to the dump to collect plastic gallon milk containers that we washed very thoroughly. We used the bottles themselves for the sap-catching pails, and cut off the handles to use as makeshift spiles. You may have heard that it takes about 100 gallons of maple sap in order to boil it down into maple syrup. I am here to tell you that was certainly our experience! The little bit of syrup that we did manage to make was wonderful though, and that winter we were able to lighten up our winter oatmeal with heavenly maple syrup. In other years we observed friends making syrup and this is a drawing I did to show a maple tapping scene using real pails instead of milk bottles!

Tapping maple sap

The Winter Thermometer

Bitter winters in the Adirondacks were difficult at best. I found myself using whatever data came my way that would help us survive. One unnerving lesson came about when I heard a loud "Crack" outside the cabin in the middle of a cold winter. At first I couldn't place it. The sound was like a gunshot but not quite. It was nighttime so I didn't go out and investigate right then, but in the morning I saw that the trunk of our maple tree had split and looked a little bit burnt. There had been no lighting storm so at first I didn't connect the sound I'd heard with the damaged tree.

Later on I found out that cold causes maple, and some other trees, to explode. One theory is that the sap, because it contains water, expands as it freezes, and causes the tree bark to split when the wood contracts as the sap expands.

Exploding maple tree

So just know that when temperatures go below freezing and you have a maple tree anywhere within hearing distance, be prepared for that loud cracking sound that is the bark of your maple tree splitting from the cold. And don't be surprised if the tree looks scorched and burnt up. You didn't miss a lightning hit, the culprit is the cold.

The Beauty of Maple Leaves

Over the years maple leaves fall, and they connect my soul to the earth. It seemed everywhere I went a fire red, or golden yellow, or orange maple leaf fell on the earth as I walked beneath the trees. As a young toddler, the leaves sounded crisp to me while I walked on the ground. As a wild three-year-old, the piles of leaves became my caves as I jumped into the mountains of raked maple leaves. Colors were my kaleidoscope and smelled so mapley earthy. The taste of maple was heaven-sent for me. From a very early age, I learned to love the stems to chew on, and I was even caught bringing them in my pockets to school. "Throw them out" were the teachers' orders. But I knew I could always get more!

Maple leaves

The streams and lakes swirled with the colors of maple leaves in the fall. Years of breathtaking colors, the trees sending the crisp sounds of their parts to the ground every fall without fail. No two leaves the same, all different! That always amazed me. I spent many a moment looking for the reddest one of all to pick up and bring inside just to look at. I often used the swing attached to the old maple in the corner of our yard, and I carved my name in a young one near the garage. In my homestead years, I learned to tap them for the luscious syrup. Many a table setting had exquisite leaves surrounding the centerpiece. A very steady, ever-changing fall reminder of nature for all of us to enjoy!

Other Maple Uses: Maple has a pleasing wood grain, and some species of maple have really beautiful grains. My father was an expert furniture maker and he used many different kinds of wood in building his highly sought-after furniture pieces. Maple was one of those woods that he used, especially bird's eye maple (the grain looks like it has bird's eyes in it), and curly maple, which has a kind of wavy pattern to it. Whole pieces of furniture are built from these two types.

As a child I used to love to go around his shop and identify the various pieces of wood that he had stacked all around. The patterns of the bird's eye and the curly maple always stood out for me, and I loved the smell of those maple pieces in particular.

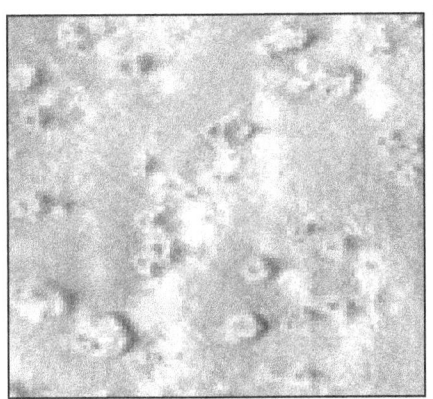 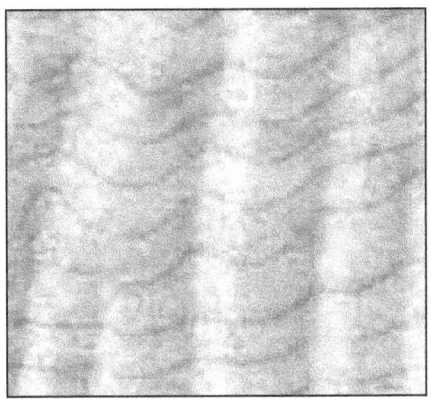

Bird's eye maple   Curly maple

At about age 5 or 6, when I realized that the delicious maple syrup came from the sap of the maple trees, well, that started my interest in what other tasty treats could be had from maple trees. I would experiment by nibbling on the stems of the leaves, and then I discovered the seeds in the wings. So the seeds of my foraging instincts began at an early age and were of very great benefit to me in my homesteading years.

A weeping willow

WILLOW

Other Names: Beaked, black, blue, weeping, Canadian, coastal plain willow. The Latin genus for the willow is *Salix*. There are over 400 different species of willow.

History: In 400 B.C., Hippocrates made a tea from the yellow leaves of the willow tree to relieve pain. Since that time, the bark of the willow tree has become known as a remedy for pain. By 1829 scientists knew that a compound called "salicin" in willow plants would give a person relief from pain. Bayer has been marketing its aspirin derived from willow bark, acetylsalicylic acid, for over 100 years. In Biblical days the willow was known as a spiritual tree, while in Elizabethan times the willow was the symbol of lost love. Eskimos used willow leaves for emergency food, and they harvested the inner bark from a type of willow, made thin strips of it, and cooked it like spaghetti. Baskets have been made from willow branches and "tendrils" since early times.

Habitat: Different species of willow can be found throughout the world, and is abundant in the cooler parts of the Northern Hemisphere. The weeping willow is a native of China, but is now found throughout North America. Willows generally are water-seeking trees, and their roots will travel underground to find available water sources, so it would be wise to not plant a willow tree anywhere near a well or a house.

Identification Characteristics of the Weeping Willow Tree: The leaves are long and narrow, not lobed, the teeth are the same size, the leaf has a short stem. The trunk of the weeping willow is somewhat short and the bark is rough and gray, but the branches are long and droopy (one reason for the

Willow leaves

name "weeping"), there are sectioned twig tendrils. The flowers (catkins) are furry. Here is a comparison between the pine cone catkin and a willow catkin.

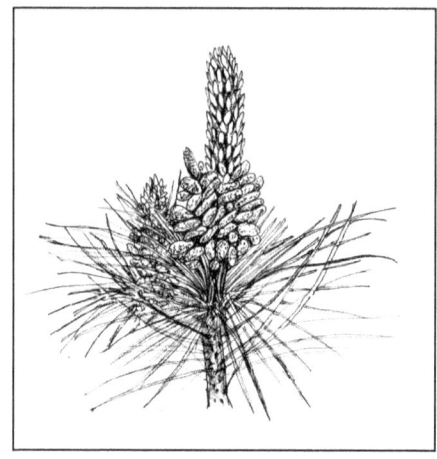

Pine catkins and new growth on top

Willow catkins

Edible Parts of the Willow Tree

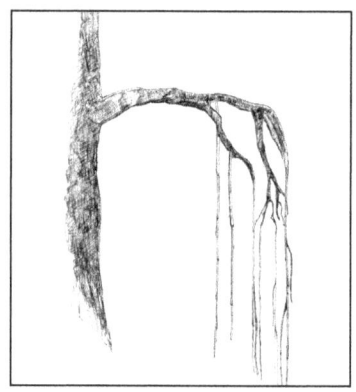

Willow "tendrils"

Willow is basically a medicine tree because of the aspirin content throughout the entire tree, so it is very important to not ingest very much of any of the parts of the tree. But if you are sure to eat or drink only small quantities, you can make willow leaf tea, and harvest, dry and store willow catkins, flowers and tendrils. Again, be sure to use sparingly. 10 to 15 catkins, or one 6 to 8 inch tendril are roughly equivalent to two aspirin.

Lesson Learned

The day was just right. Warm but not hot and the catkins were yellow against the weeping willow branches. Perfect day to make a large willow basket. New York City outlets had asked for them in late winter. I began by pulling down on a bunch of tendrils. I piled the tendrils (2 to 8 feet long) next to the tree and when I had enough, I began to make the basket. Settling with my back against the willow tree, I began to strip the tendrils to a smooth finish. The yellow catkins were falling off as fast as the leaves. I loved the sweet catkin odor and began to ingest a few here and there. Two hours later I had almost completed the basket and had eaten probably a cup and a half of yellow catkins.

Making willow baskets under the willow tree.

Time to stand up and find the special tendril that would become the handle. I fell right over because I was dizzy and faint. My friends observed this and came running out to the field where I lay on the ground. After a long hour of me drinking a lot of water, we determined I had probably eaten too much natural willow aspirin and as a result had all the side effects—headache, dizziness, ringing in my ears, not to mention the unfinished basket that didn't have its handle.

Next day I slowly walked back to the tree, located and picked my special handle tendril of willow, and inserted it into the side of the basket to complete the handle. I learned a big lesson that day about why you don't ever eat very much of the willow parts so you can avoid the aspirin effects. In this case the rule of eating a small amount must be followed.

<u>Willow Wreaths</u>: In addition to making willow tendril baskets I would also make willow tendril wreaths. You can make the entire wreath with the willow leaves on, or you can strip off the leaves and just use the tendrils to make the wreath. And then there's a combination that I would do, which was to use a leafy branch at the outer edge of the wreath and then weave the striped tendril in and out to completely circle the wreath. This created a nice effect. Willow wreaths are not only nice to look at, but you can later wash the dust off them and eat one tendril for a bit of natural pain relief as well.

Willow wreaths and fronds

From the Ridiculous to the Sublime!

I was very miserable six weeks before one Christmas because of some shoulder surgery I'd had. I had really overdone it and overused my shoulders from hard work. So here I sat, a normally very active person, in my cabin bed going stir crazy because I could only use my hands, and not lift my shoulders at all. I knew without a doubt that I would not be very happy for the next several holiday weeks before Christmas, and was feeling pretty sorry for myself. I was so uncomfortable in my body, and besides which I was trying to get over the shock of having to be in a hospital for that painful experience in the first place. Well, that shock was nothing compared to the one I got from a single phone call on a day that had started out so miserably. Of all the places I certainly did not expect to get a phone call from, Lord and Taylors topped the list. My husband had brought me the news that they had called me, and that I should contact their New York City office and find out what they needed.

Oh, joy! They wanted me to make 67 little "backpack" baskets, each about 3 inches tall, to hold a tiny vase with a flowering rose in it. They would then attach the little rose basket decorations onto the branches of a balsam Christmas tree about 3 1/2 feet tall. Could I make the baskets? Now, how strange and wonderful is that? I couldn't use my shoulders for a few weeks before Christmas, so just about anything else I considered doing for the holiday season I couldn't do, and this was one of the very few projects I actually could do. I checked with my medical people, and the nurses and doctors loved the idea, so I said, "Yes!" and got to work. My husband brought me the willow tendrils that I would need to weave the baskets from, and I used a thin strip of birch bark to trim the top of each basket rim.

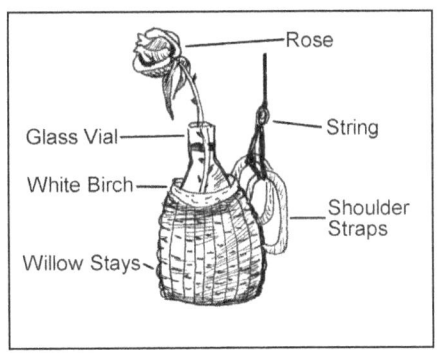

The parts of my willow basket

One of 67 baskets

The project kept me busy for two weeks. I had so much fun doing it, and it was such a help in taking my mind off my body situation. We mailed the baskets off to Lord and Taylors and when we received the paid bill, they let us know they thought the baskets were gorgeous. They had worked perfectly as holders for the roses on the tree centerpiece they displayed right inside their front door throughout that Christmas season.

And so to this day I have this wonderful Christmas memory of how a timely and much appreciated phone call turned things around for me during a low period in my life.

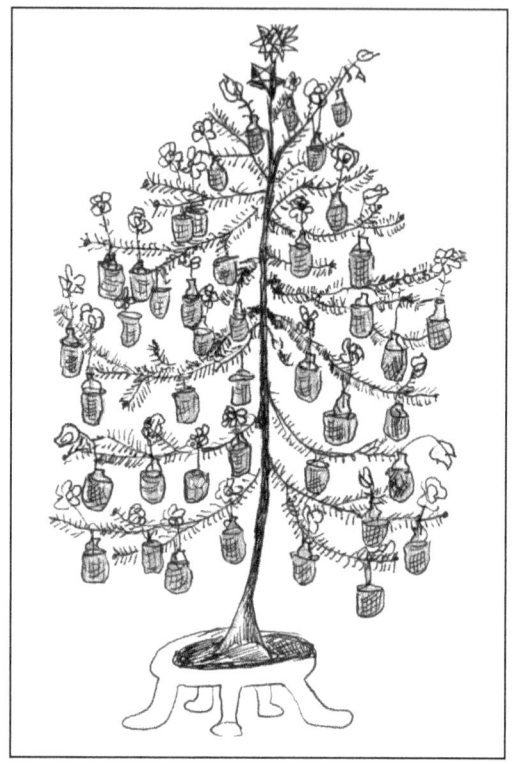

Christmas tree of roses in willow baskets

Other Uses: Willow is grown for fuel, and also to produce charcoal, brooms, chairs, toys, whistles, wicker for basket weaving. It is also included in cosmetics in combination with other ingredients in astringents, lotions, facials, creams, and anti-aging products. The wood from the white willow is made into paper pulp, while the best charcoal for artists' crayons is from the white willow.

Medicinal Uses: As an aspirin. Willow sprouts in the spring make a very medicinal tonic. But remember: 10 to 15 catkins, or one 6 to 8 inch tendril are roughly equivalent to two aspirin, so use with care.

Willow Catkins

Young Beech tree

BEECH

Other Names: Carolina beech, gray, red, stone, white, winter beech. The American Beech is *Fagus grandifolia* and is the only species of beech tree in North America. The European beech is *Fagus sylvatica*.

History: According to some historians, the first written European literature was in Sanskit on beech bark. In American colonial times, the leaves were used to stuff mattresses, and the wood was used for furniture and tools. The wood of this tree is still used to build furniture, and additionally, flooring, plywood, paper, and railroad ties. Because the bark is so smooth, it seems to encourage people to carve their initials into it, and for many years there was a beech tree in Tennessee that had Daniel Boone's name carved on it.

Habitat: The American beech can be found in rich, moist soils, and in forest areas.

Identification Characteristics of the American Beech Tree: Smooth, grayish and white bark. The roots of beech show above the ground in some areas. The oval-shaped leaves, 2 to about 5 inches, are alternative. The twigs of the beech are very thin and slender, the buds look kind of like long thorns. The flowers are small and yellow and clustered together, and grow into prickly burrs which contain edible fruit (nuts). The tree grows to about 80 feet and can live 400 years.

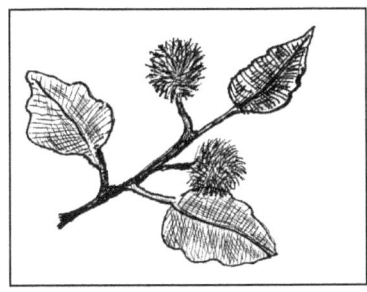
Beech leaves and burrs

Beech burrs, shells, nuts

Beech burrs

Edible Parts of the Beech Tree

Leaves. Twigs, and Nuts: Leaves can be picked and put into salads, twigs for munching, and the nuts inside the burrs are edible. I would open the burrs and then soak the two halves for a couple of hours. You can press them into a pesto.

Recipe for Italian Beech Leaves:

Ingredients: 2 cups young beech leaves, springs or twigs. 3/4 cup water, 1 clove garlic, 1 tablespoon olive oil. Combine all ingredients in a saucepan and simmer for 8 minutes. Serve as an appetizer or garnish. Note: This recipe can be adapted to beech buds, white and yellow birch buds, young birch leaves, or young maple leaves and seeds.

Beech Nuts in the Saw Mill

We lived near a saw mill for some years, and on this particular morning I didn't have too much to do. I had my food already prepared for the day and because it was so warm and sunny, I wandered over to the mill and watched the work being done there. Whenever I entered the mill it was always from the side door and then I would be only a few feet from the trimmer saw man, my husband Ken. I was careful not to distract any of the workers because it was dangerous near those sharp saws, and because of steel flying through the air.

The job of the "picker", who had a long grapling hook kind of like a harpoon, was to pull the sides of bark off the wood if they got hung up in the cutting process. During the cutting process, often wood knots would roll out of the sawed pieces and I was able to take those knots home to make things out of them, like hand carved bowls. On this day that I was there some very large beech logs were loaded on and were pushed into the saw blade one at a time. A slab of bark rolled off and was pushed into the holding area under the saw. Then I saw it! A very big, two to three foot hole opened in the tree and out tumbled literally a whole year's supply of beech nuts collected by squirrels! The sawyer looked at me, stopped the saw, and it ground to a slow spin. "They're all yours," he said.

Beech nut bonanza!

I grabbed a very large leather tote bag and ran to the pile of nuts and filled that bag up. It was way too heavy for me so I left it for Ken to bring home, and it was like Christmas! My next many hours were spent hoarding beech nuts in containers. We finally had enough beech nuts for a year or so of toasting them slightly in a fry pan over the campfire. What a wonderful feeling!

Other Uses: Because beech is a high density wood it is made into pulp, charcoal, and is favored as a fuel wood. Drum sets can be made from beech. Beech nut oil is used in cooking and as a salad oil, and cheeses smoked on beech wood have a unique and desirable flavor. In France the nuts from the European beech are roasted, ground, and served as a coffee substitute.

TREE ACTIVITIES

The following are just suggestions of interesting tree activities you can do with younger people. Of course create your own games, and have the students make up activities too.

1. Collect photos of the trees in this book and have the students identify them. You could do this as a flash card game by giving each child a color photograph of a tree from a magazine or other source to cut out and paste or tape onto a piece of cardboard. The name of the tree gets written on the back. Put all the cards in a stack and have the children correctly identify all the trees in the entire stack.

Flash Card Game

2. In the spring, if you are in an area where you can do this, go outside and find examples of trees discussed in this book. For a maple, birch or beech tree, pull down a branch to show the student a new bud. For an evergreen, show what a catkin looks

like. Have the student find another such tree and show you the bud or catkin. Take some of each home with you, plus some branches and twigs, and prepare something with your harvest, such as tea, a stir fry, or twig popsicles.

3. Later in the spring show the student the different leaves and needles, and bring some home. Have the student put the leaves on paper and trace the shape as closely as possible, especially the teeth at the edge of the leaf.

4. Then in the fall, take a look at the leaves and needles and have the student notice the similarities and the differences from early spring to the fall. Also gather balsam, willow and pine branches and twigs to make into wreaths or other holiday decorations. This is really an opportunity to get very creative!

5. Take photos of the trees as they change through the months of the seasons and at the end of the calendar year, make a calendar for the next year that shows how trees change. The Fall months should be especially colorful!

6. For any of the trees that are not in your immediate vicinity, do some research at your library or on the internet and find out which edible trees are in your area and where they are. Then go and see them, and forage from them if you have permission. Also find out about more trees that have edible parts than the ones that have been covered in this book.

7. Find out if anyone would like to do a school presentation about edible trees and help them set that up.

8. Go around your house and find all the things that are made from wood. Make a list. (Thanks Holly Drake for 8, 9 & 12!)

9. Visit a nursery and find out the best way to plant your own tree. Bring the potted tree home and plant it. (Get help with this if needed.) Start a notebook on growing your tree, make drawings of your tree, and stories about it, and take pictures every year of you next to your tree.

10. Find a nice tree area and have the students do paintings of trees. Then have an art show.

11. Research the art of whittling and then experiment with different woods to find ones that would be easy to whittle. Probably your local lumber yard will have pieces they would be willing to give you for such a project.

12. Make leaf T shirts. Use a solid colored T shirt for this activity. Collect a variety of leaves from trees. Fill a spray bottle with an ounce of Clorox bleach and fill the rest of the way with water. Stuff a piece of cardboard between the shirt front and back. Lay out the leaves in a pattern or design that is pleasing, hold them in place with small rocks. Try placing a leaf or two over the shoulder and down the sleeve as well. Spray the shirt with bleach and leave in the sunshine. After an hour or so, when the shirt is dry, remove the rocks and leaves. Where the leaves had been is now the original color of the t shirt and the rest is bleached. Take a picture of you in your new T-shirt.

13. Look at the drawing below and identify each of the trees.

FORAGING RULES FOR EDIBLE TREES

Be sure to follow each of these rules carefully.

1. Do not forage trees that are closer than 200 feet from a road.

2. Never collect from areas sprayed with herbicides, pesticides, or other chemicals.

3. Positively identify all trees you intend to ingest as food or medicine. Use 3 photographic references whenever possible.

4. Roll a tiny bit of the leaf between your fingers and sniff. Does this smell good? Then, run that tiny bit of plant on your gums. Wait 20 minutes. Look for burning, numbing, nausea, itching, or stinging.

5. If no reaction, take another bit of leaf, pour a cup of boiling water over it to make a weak tea and drink slowly, over a period of 20 minutes. Check for signs of irritation.

6. People with allergies should bruise up a piece of leaf, and place on inner arm using a band aid and wait for several hours. If your skin has no redness, process with a small amount of plant.

7. Keep all tree samples away from children, pets, etc.

8. Teach children to keep all plants out of their mouths.

9. Avoid smoke from burning plants or trees.

10. Call and report chemical spills resulting in contaminated areas.

11. Keep tree parts in separate bags when foraging and collecting.

Eat the Trees!
Study Guide

The purpose of this guide is to provide research and activity actions for *Eat the Trees!*, so you can gain practical application of the material. The steps are designed to help you have successful and rewarding tree foraging experiences. You are encouraged to do as many of the steps as makes sense to do, and to add additional individual actions for personal benefit. For any steps that are not possible to do because of the time of year, or your location, etc., save them to do at the appropriate time. This Study Guide can also serve as the basis for teacher lesson plans on tree foraging education.

If any confusions arise as to the meaning of the text in the book or in these steps, check to see if there are any words that are not clearly understood, and look up the definitions in a good dictionary.

It is suggested that the steps be done in order, for best application of the materials.

Introductory Material

1. READ: *Eat the Trees!*, section "Disclaimer".

2. RESEARCH: Find out the state and local regulations regarding foraging trees in your area, if you plan to harvest beyond your own home area.

3. READ: "Preface".

4. ACTIVITY: Work out for yourself your purpose and goals for learning about edible wild foods.

5. READ: "Introduction".

6. ACTIVITY: Think of any pleasant moments that you have

had that involve trees. If you want to, make a drawing or a painting of a tree or trees, or write an essay or a poem about a tree.

Chapter One: PINE

1. READ: Section "Other Names" up to "Identification Characteristics of the Pine Tree".

2. RESEARCH:

   a) Find out why trees have Latin names.

   b) Learn more about the Algonquian Indians, and how they used the pine tree.

   c) Find out what types of pine tree are in your local area.

3. ACTIVITY: Go to a store and see if you can find some pine nuts for sale. Health food stores usually have them, and many regular food stores do too.

4. READ: Section "Identification Characteristics of the Pine Tree".

5. ACTIVITY:

   a) Look at real pine needles and pine cones, or find some pictures of them.

   b) Locate some deciduous trees near you. Notice the difference between the needles and cones of the pine tree, and the leaves of the deciduous tree. (If it is winter time, find color photos of the trees.)

6. READ: Section "Your Foraging Equipment".

7. RESEARCH: For any of the items mentioned that you don't already have and think you might need, find places where you can get your foraging equipment so you are fully prepared.

8. READ: "Foraging Rules for Edible Trees" on page 69. Be sure you understand why each rule is there.

9. ACTIVITY: Make your own list of the foraging rules so that you will have it with you whenever you are out foraging trees. Add your own personal ones.

10. READ: Section "Edible Parts of the Pine Tree", 'Catkins' and 'Needles'.

11. ACTIVITY: Find some catkins (if it is spring) and some pine needles. Notice the resemblance of the catkins to caterpillars. Twist the needles and taste the center of them to have the pine taste. Or look online for images.

12. READ: Section "Inner Bark" up to "A Note on Tree Roots".

13. ACTIVITY:

a) Make your own drawing of the sections of the pine tree layers. Be sure to label the layers, and notice where the inner bark and sapwood layers are.

b) Before you go to forage any trees, work out what you want to harvest from the trees and how you will transport your items home.

c) Find a pine tree that is permissible for you to forage from, and cut a small branch off. Locate the inner bark layer.

14. READ: Sections "A Note on Tree Roots" up to "Grinding Inner Bark to Flour".

15. ACTIVITY:

a) Figure out your drying, storing, and labeling procedures for the edible pine parts you will have.

b) Decide on the immediate uses of pine parts that you want

73

to have when you bring freshly foraged pine parts home (sun tea, pine needle tea, popsicles, ice cubes, etc.) and have the containers available.

c) After you have brought home your pine tree edibles, find recipes that include pine tree parts as ingredients (as in Linda Runyon's *The Essential Wild Food Survival Guide*, "Part III: Wild Food Recipes"), or create your own recipes!

16. READ: Section "Grinding Inner Bark to Flour".

17. RESEARCH:

a) If you plan to grind inner tree bark to flour, be sure that you have or can acquire a blender such as a Vita-Mixer that will grind the bark into a fine enough flour that can be used for baking. Or research the grinders mentioned in this section so you can have one that will do the job.

b) Before you bake with the pine flour, figure out additional non-plant flours that you might want to use to combine with the pine flour for your baked product.

18. READ: Section "Gathering Pine Tree Sap".

19. ACTIVITY: If you are planning to gather sap from a pine tree, collect ahead of time the items you will need to do it.

20. READ: Section "Nutritional Value for Pine Nuts" to the end of the Pine chapter.

21. RESEARCH:

a) See if your local health food store carries Pycnogenol, and any cough syrups made from white pine sap. Ask if they have other products that are based on pine elements.

b) Go to a local furniture store and find some pieces that are built from pine.

c) Find additional items (toys, containers, shelving, frames, puzzles, etc.) made from pine.

22. ACTIVITY: Get a piece of pine from someplace like a lumber supply store and build something from pine.

Chapter Two: BIRCH

1. READ: Sections "Other Names" up to "Identification Characteristics of the Birch Tree".

2. RESEARCH:

a) If you can, locate a birch tree and feel the bark of the trunk and notice the papery peels.

b) Feel the toothed edges of a leaf.

c) Find out about other types of birch trees and where they are located.

3. READ: Section "Edible Parts of the Birch Tree" up to "Collecting Birch Sap".

4. ACTIVITY:

a) Make your own list of the edible parts of the birch tree, and note why you should be careful to only eat a small amount.

b) Locate a bottle of aspirin and look at the ingredients.

5. READ: Section "Collecting Birch Sap".

6. ACTIVITY: Make a drawing of the steps you would take to show how you would go about tapping a birch tree. Include a container that you could use to catch the sap, and what you could use for a spile.

7. READ: Sections "Nutritional Value for Birch Leaves" to "Birch Survival Strips".

8. ACTIVITIES:

a) Decide on the birch parts you would like to forage and bring home, and figure out how you could do that, and how you could store and prepare your birch parts. If you don't now have a place set aside for firewood but plan to have a fireplace and firewood for winter, work out how you will acquire the wood and where you will store it.

b) If you are artistic or know somebody who is, plan on saving birch branches that you or they can cut cut into disks and draw on, and possibly sell. Then go to a souvenir store and see if it sells any wood items that are in a natural condition.

c) Find out how the store decides which local wood products it will sell. If possible, go visit an artist who makes items out of wood to sell. You could also attend craft fairs and local fairs and see what they have.

9. READ: Section "Birch Survival Strips".

10. ACTIVITY: Get some birch branches and follow the steps of peeling the birch layers so that you get layers that you can cut into strips and make into survival packets.

11. READ: Sections: "Other Birch Tree Uses" and "Medicinal Uses".

12. ACTIVITY:

a) Chew on a birch twig and experience the hint of sap flavor.

b) See if you can find birch beer in a store or for sale on the internet.

Chapter Three: BALSAM FIR

1. READ: Sections "Other Names" up to "Edible Parts of the Balsam Fir Tree".

2. RESEARCH:

   a) If you can, locate a balsam fir tree and feel the needles.

   b) Find out where some Christmas tree farms are located. If there are any near you, go and visit the farm and find out some information about how the trees are planted, which kinds, and how they are raised and sold.

3. READ: Sections "Edible Parts of the Balsam Fir Tree" to "The Smell of the Forest".

4. ACTIVITY:

   a) For any edible parts of balsam firs that you might harvest, consider ahead of time how you will store and prepare your foods so you are prepared for that when you bring home your bounty.

   b) When the holiday season arrives, identify which decorated Christmas trees in your area are balsam firs and which are pine trees.

   c) Decide if you want to make some seasonal edible wreaths for yourself and as gifts, and plan how you will gather the materials you will need for that.

5. READ: Sections "The Smell of the Forest" and "Winter Camping Survival".

6. RESEARCH: If you are interested in starting or being a part of a cottage industry and spreading the word about wild food, find out what the state and local requirements are to do that in your area. Find out if there are cottage industries near you that you could visit, to get an idea of how that would work. There may be Farmer's Markets to visit as well, for more data on how to sell your products locally.

7. ACTIVITY: If you are considering winter camping, review

the survival actions given and work out everything you should do, and what you will need, to have a successful experience.

8. READ: Sections "Other Balsam Fir Uses" and "Medicinal Uses".

9. RESEARCH: See if you can find medicinal ointments, oils, or other products that contain as a component the oil from the balsam resin.

10. ACTIVITY: If you have a balsam fir near you, notice when the sap blisters form on the trunk in the spring, so that if you need to get some sap for a wound in a hurry you will know where to get it.

Chapter Four: MAPLE

1. READ: Sections "Other Names" to "Edible Parts of the Maple Tree".

2. RESEARCH: Find locally or on the internet or in books, color examples of the maple leaf in spring and fall.

3. ACTIVITY: If you have maple trees near you, take a look at the fall foliage and notice the various colors of the leaves. Decide on your own activity that you want to do with fall maple leaves.

4. READ: Sections "Edible Parts of the Maple Tree" to "The Maple Sap Saga".

5. RESEARCH:

   a) Be sure you can identify the early maple leaf buds. When spring comes, decide if you want to harvest them and be prepared to do that, and to store and prepare them to eat.

   b) If they are in season, find some maple seed helicopters. If they aren't, make sure that you know how to identify the helicopter wings so that when the time comes and you have maple trees in your area, you can forage the seeds from the wings.

6. ACTIVITY: If you have collected maple seeds, make some maple seed cakes and see what you think about them.

7. READ: Sections "The Maple Sap Saga" to the end of the chapter.

8. RESEARCH:

a) Find out if there are people locally who have maple trees that they are or will be tapping for maple syrup. If possible, have the tree owners go through their process with you on how they do it. If you are not in such an area, see if you can find a video on the internet of somebody who is successfully tapping maples for syrup.

b) Go see some maple wood before it has been made into furniture, and then look at maple furniture pieces. Notice the grain of the wood.

9. ACTIVITY: Chew on some maple stems that you have harvested and see if you can detect the maple flavor.

Chapter Five: WILLOW

1. READ: Sections "Other Names" to "Edible Parts of the Willow Tree".

2. RESEARCH:

a) Find a weeping willow tree near you, or locate a picture of one. Notice the shape of the leaves and the way the branches droop towards the ground.

b) Look at the ingredients of a bottle of aspirin.

3. READ: Section "Edible Parts of the Willow Tree".

4. ACTIVITY: Review the equivalents to aspirin for willow catkins and tendrils, and why you should not exceed them.

5. READ: Sections "Lesson Learned" to the end of the chapter.

6. RESEARCH: If you plan to make wreaths from tree parts, research to find out if there are also wild edible plants that you might want to include in your wreaths. Be sure to have all of the parts for your wreath collected together before you start making them.

7. ACTIVITY: If you have access to a willow tree, collect some "tendrils" and see if you can weave your own basket. If this is an activity that you enjoy, think about making your own small baskets to hold flowers or plants.

Chapter Six: Beech

1. READ: Sections "Other Names" to "Edible Parts of the Beech Tree".

2. RESEARCH: Find a beech tree near you, or locate a picture of one. Notice the shape of the leaves and the smooth bark.

3. ACTIVITY:

   a) If you have a beech tree nearby, feel the prickly burrs, and then open them to find the nuts inside.

   b) There are five beech burrs in the photograph. See if you can locate them all.

4. READ: Section "Edible Parts of the Beech Tree" to "Beech Nuts in the Saw Mill".

5. ACTIVITY: If you harvest beech nuts, try the recipe for Italian beech leaves. Or, harvest some birch or maple leaves and try the recipe with them.

6. READ: Sections "Beech Nuts in the Saw Mill" to the end of the chapter.

7. RESEARCH:

a) See if you can find out how the name of the Beech-Nut baby food company got its name.

b) Discover if there are U.S. companies making coffee from beech nuts. If so, and if you have access to beech nuts and you have a sturdy grinder, see if you can make some beech nut coffee.

Chapter Seven: Tree Activities

1. READ: Review all of the items listed in this chapter.

2. ACTIVITY:

a) Pick out activities to do yourself, or with children.

b) Have the children come up with their own tree activities to do.

FINAL ACTIVITY: Review what you have learned about foraging trees for food, and make sure that you have worked out how you will go about foraging, harvesting, transporting, storing and preparing edible tree parts.

Praise for *Eat the Trees!*

Linda Runyon's book *Eat the Trees!* will become a wonderful asset to all survivalists and campers alike. It encompasses historical uses, medicinal as well as nutritional value, and the viability of filling the stomachs of families as they forge the wilds for either a greater peace, or simply an easier and better way of life. The book gives viability in thriving on natural foods of the earth, whether it be in times of want or simply to enjoy free forest edibles.

As time marches on, this book will remain in the hands of those who chose to carry the essence of life into the next generation and provide for our posterity despite world agricultural situations. For out of the wilds of the earth, man came to be and flourished, not by commercial farming and industrial processing, but by foraging for all his daily needs.

It's a time for back-to-basics in living, walking on from the irradiated foods, added chemicals, increased hormones and genetic altering. As man finds himself reverting to a more natural state through global tension and strife, the circle of life takes him to wonderful wild edibles of the field and forest which God so intended, many millennia ago.

With Linda's fountain of information on wild tree edibles, this spark of light can be shown around the world for those who indeed seek after a healthier and cheaper way of living while ultimately giving latter-day man Life.

—*Jean Selman, survivalist, wild food enthusiast*

I love that Linda has thought to extend the usefulness of this book's information by creating a study guide. The educational potential of each chapter is maximized with additional studies of outside resources relating to that chapter's topic. And the suggested activities are a great way to break each section down into simple goals to achieve one at a time. A perfectly enjoyable supplement to any curriculum!

As a parent, I appreciate that for the most part *Eat the Trees!* is written in a manner that would be very interesting for children to read. Not too scientific, but very personalized (with stories) and exciting as well as informative.

Linda's very thorough explanations of how to properly gather the edible part of trees and what to do with the harvest makes me want to grab a bag of supplies and head out into the woods with my children to put these foraging methods to the test! What a great way to teach kids survival skills, as well as a greater appreciation for their environment and the plants all around us!

—Kendra Plummons, radio host, parent,
NewLifeOnAHomestead.com

After reading this remarkable book I was propelled outside to find each tree and harvest its gifts. Being a forager for edible plants, I usually look down at leaf shapes to see what wild food is available . . . now I'm looking up! Linda has lit yet another 'wild fire' and I will never be the same. Trees are such an amazing gift because they offer so much food all in one place! Even though I've heard of these offerings, it was not till reading this book that I feel educated enough to go 'eat a tree'. She answers every question, the illustrations are wonderful and her humorous tree stories are delightful. This is another MUST HAVE Linda Runyon book!

—Holly Drake, wild food consultant and chef,
WildBlessings.com

The trees and the weeds are always with us and thanks to Linda Runyon and other pioneers of modern foraging, are an instant and ready food supply in a pinch and always handy to enhance nutrition.

Linda's writing style and her combination of story telling and instruction make *Eat the Trees!* a delightful read and a treasure of survival wisdom. Her vast knowledge and experience with wild food and her keen instincts make this little book a timely and essential work.

Eat the Trees! may well be the first book of its kind and provides us with crucial information at a perilous time in history. This newest of Linda's works, together with her *Essential Wild Food Survival Guide*, are vital resources for every household, especially in these uncertain times.

—Steve Arnold, forager,
permaculture enthusiast

About the Author

Linda Runyon lived with her son and husband in the Adirondacks of upstate NY for 13 years without indoor plumbing, electricity or running water. This wilderness experience of homesteading on the outskirts of remote Indian Lake forced Linda to find the knowledge and skills to live from the land.

For many years after leaving the woods, Linda taught thousands and a generation of wild food teachers to identify, find, harvest, prepare, store & use wild edible food. She continues still to teach through her books, cards, video and website. She still enriches her life with these skills, even during her residence in a comfortable retirement community.

www.ingramcontent.com/pod-product-compliance
Lightning Source LLC
Chambersburg PA
CBHW032058150426
43194CB00006B/576